The editors would like to thank
BARBARA KIEFER, Ph.D.,
Charlotte S. Huck Professor of Children's Literature,
The Ohio State University, and
SCOT BORG, Ph.D., RENEE CRAIN, KELLY K. FALKNER, Ph.D.,
ANNA KERTTULA-ECHAVE, Ph.D., SUSAN KLINKHAMMER,
ROBERTA MARINELLI, Ph.D., WINIFRED REUNING, and JENNIFER THOMPSON
of the Office of Polar Programs,
National Science Foundation,
for their assistance in the preparation of this book.

Visit us on the Web!
www.randomhouse.com/kids
www.seussville.com

Educators and librarians, for a variety of teaching tools, visit us at
www.randomhouse.com/teachers

Library of Congress Cataloging-in-Publication Data
Worth, Bonnie.
Ice is nice! : all about the North and South Poles / by Bonnie Worth ;
illustrated by Aristides Ruiz and Joe Mathieu. — 1st ed.
  p. cm. — (The cat in the hat's learning library)
ISBN 978-0-375-82885-0 (trade) — ISBN 978-0-375-92885-7 (lib. bdg.)
1. Arctic regions—Discovery and exploration—Juvenile literature.
2. North Pole—Discovery and exploration—Juvenile literature.
3. South Pole—Discovery and exploration—Juvenile literature.
I. Ruiz, Aristides, ill. II. Mathieu, Joseph, ill. III. Title.
G614.W 67 2010
910.911—dc22
2009025072

Printed in the United States of America   10 9 8 7 6 5 4 3 2 1   First Edition

Ice Is Nice!

by Bonnie Worth

illustrated by Aristides Ruiz and Joe Mathieu

The Cat in the Hat's Learning Library®

Random House 🏠 New York

I'm the Cat in the Hat
and we're off and away
to visit the poles—North
and South—in one day.

It will be a quick trip
in the SS *Ice Chopper*—
my Super Slip-Sliding
Ice-Breaking Pole Hopper.

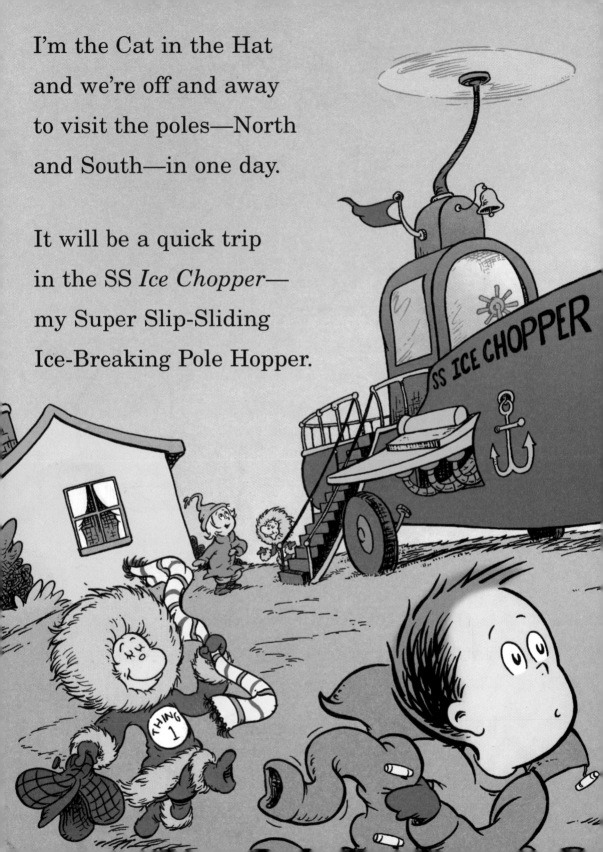

The North Pole will be
the Pole Hopper's first stop.
It's the farthest point north
on the earth. It's the top!

Some call this the Land
of the Midnight Sun.
What's wrong
with this statement?
Show us, Thing One.

To call this a land is
an incorrect notion:
the North Pole is located
in the Arctic Ocean!

WELCOME
TO THE LAND OF THE
MIDNIGHT SUN!

Over most of this ocean
sea ice is floating.
So only icebreakers
are good here for boating.

Snow on land near here
can pile up quite thickly,
forming ice caps and glaciers
that do not move quickly.

If you sit and watch
and you wait patiently,
icebergs will split off
and spill into the sea.

Icebergs are big
and a danger to ships—
much thicker than the sea ice
our icebreaker flips.

I have asked widely
and I have been told
some very good reasons
the Arctic's so cold.

Earth spins on an axis
that goes through its middle,
making one turn a day—
that's one part of the riddle.

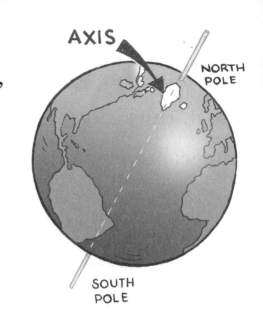

On the side of the earth
that is facing away
from the sun, it is night—
on the other side, day.

Earth spins on its axis
while circling the sun.
It takes a full year
till this orbit is done.

Six months the North Pole
tips away from sun's light
and makes Arctic winter—
one very looooong night.

In the summer up north,
when light shines night and day,
white snow everywhere
reflects sunlight away.

Without light, it's COLD!
Sometimes eighty below.
That means eighty degrees
less than good old zero.

WINTER

DAY

AUTUMN

Native peoples live here.
You ask, are they nuts?
In the past, they kept snug
in their sturdy skin huts.

Today people live here
like you and like me,
with houses and cell phones
and color TV.

Some still fish and hunt but not in dogsleds. Those marks in the snow are a snowmobile's treads!

And this group of people that you can see here are nomads who follow their herd of reindeer.

Adaptation is the word,
I have been told,
for how Arctic animals
weather the cold.

Seals, whales, and walruses
have blubber, you see.
These layers of fat
keep them warm as can be.

BLUBBER

The snowy owl's warm
in a feathered snowsuit.
Thing One's wearing one.
Aw, now, isn't he cute?

This shaggy musk ox
has a coat of fine fur.
That coat keeps him warm.
Wish I had one . . . brrrrr!

I will say this to you—
and I think it is fair—
that the king of this pole
is the great polar bear.

He has layers of blubber
and fur that is white.
But his skin is as black
as the dark of the night.

The polar bear has
an unusual hide.
It is made up of hairs
that are hollow inside.

POLAR BEAR HAIR

This skin and hair
just cannot be beat
for absorbing the sun's rays
and holding the heat.

As he walks on the snow
on four snowshoe-like paws,
no animal's safe
from a polar bear's claws.

In winter the foxes
blend into the snow.
White fur camouflages
them quite well, you know.

They hide in the snow
and hope that they may
sneak around that old bear
and live one more day.

Winter year-round?
Oh my, what a bummer!
But for four months you'll find
there is actually summer.

In summer, the North Pole
tilts back toward sun's light.
It is sunny all day,
even when it's midnight.

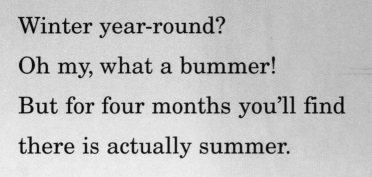

It gets a bit warmer.
The snow melts in patches.
A tiny insect called
the midge fly now hatches.

Berries and mosses
and all kinds of flowers,
when temperatures rise,
are sprouting in hours.

Summers bring heat
up to eighty degrees.
Walk outside with no hat
and you won't even freeze.

The owl and the fox
turn brown like the hare
and blend into the land
when it is warm there.

This place can get lively—
it's true, mark my words—
when the caribou come
by the thousands in herds.

They've come many miles.
It's called a migration.
They give birth on the way.
It's no spring vacation.

They've come north to graze
as long as it's warm
and head south before
the first autumn storm.

Speaking of south,
it's high time we hop.
The South Pole will be
the Pole Hopper's next stop.

While the North Pole
is found in the water, you see,
the South Pole's on land,
and take it from me:

ATLANTIC OCEAN

ANTARCTICA

PACIFIC OCEAN

INDIAN OCEAN

SOUTH
POLE

Antarctica's valleys
and its mountains steep
are buried in ice that's
at least two miles deep!

One look at this chart
in my hand will make clear,
when it's summer up north
it is winter down here.

If you thought that the north
was a cold place to be,
the south can get colder
by far, believe me.

SUMMER

NORTH
POLE

SOUTH
POLE

WINTER

Minus 130 degrees!
And this is no laugh—
it's so cold I just snapped
my ski pole in half!

It's colder down south,
and the main reason why
is these mountains that rise
up a mile or two high.

Summer's cold too,
but penguins come still
to eat the fat shrimp
and the plentiful krill.

Emperor penguins
stay near the coast.
Small fish and shrimp are
what they like most.

KRILL

And there's nothing here
good for making a nest.
So fathers' warm feet
cradle their chicks' eggs best.

They raise their chicks
in a crèche all together.
They huddle to stay warm
in the freezing weather.

But emperor penguins
are only one kind.
Other penguins come here,
as you will soon find.

Chinstrap penguins,
most numerous of all,
live in large groups
and have a shrill call.

Adélie penguins
also live in large flocks.
Mates watch over eggs
in nests lined with rocks.

A head stripe's the sign
of the gentoo breed,
the penguin with the fastest
underwater speed.

Whatever great height
the rockhoppers may lack,
they make up in pluck
and are quick to attack.

Penguins of all kinds
get here on ice floes
because penguins can't fly,
as everyone knows.

They have stubby legs
and waddle, you know.
They bob back and forth
and the going is slow.

But way down deep
in these Antarctic seas,
the penguins can swim
with the greatest of ease.

Have you heard of this thing
that is called climate change?
It means the earth's temperatures
are shifting in range.

The earth's getting warmer,
and the polar ice
is melting quite quickly,
which isn't so nice.

Students and scientists from dozens of nations are studying the poles from ships, planes, and stations.

Their satellites watch the weather and ice. They track climate change and check their facts twice!

If we all work together,
I hope in my heart
we can keep our poles icy
or make a good start!

GLOSSARY

Axis: An imaginary pole or line running through the earth, around which it spins.

Camouflage: A way that animals and plants are disguised for self-protection.

Climate change: The increase in the earth's temperature in the past century, which affects the climate and the ice at the poles.

Continent: One of the eight landmasses on the earth.

Crèche: A large group of baby animals being cared for by adults; from a French word that means *crib*.

Nomads: A group of people who have no fixed home and who wander in search of food or grazing land for their herds.

Plentiful: In large amounts.

FOR FURTHER READING

Face to Face with Polar Bears by Norbert Rosing and Elizabeth Carney (National Geographic Children's Books). Fantastic photographs and information about polar bears! For preschool–grade 3.

Houses of Snow, Skin and Bones by Bonnie Shemie (Tundra Books). While most Inuit now live in modern houses, this is a fascinating look at more traditional native dwellings. For grades 2–5.

Mama, Do You Love Me? by Barbara M. Joosse, illustrated by Barbara Lavallee (Chronicle Books). A simple, beautifully illustrated story about an Inuit mother and her daughter. A great introduction to a different culture. For grades 3 and up.

Penguins by Seymour Simon (Collins, Smithsonian Institution). An award-winning science writer investigates penguins. For preschool–grade 3.

The Top and Bottom of the World by Allan Fowler (Children's Press, Rookie Read-About Science). All about the climate and animal life at the North and South Poles. For preschool–grade 3.

INDEX